ARE YOU PROFITABLE
TO YOUR PASTOR?

By Byron D. August

Are You Profitable to Your Pastor?
By Byron D. August
ISBN 0-9673727-1-2
Copyright © 2000 by
Ready For The World Ministries
P. O. Box 2833
Broken Arrow, OK 74013

Editorial Consultant: Cynthia Hansen
Cover Design: Dennis Whitley
Text Design: Lisa Simpson

Contents

Preface

The purpose of this book is to inspire men and women to become profitable to their pastors. A strong local church can only be built when strong individuals rise up to support the man or woman God has called to lead that particular congregation.

Today many people feel that missionaries are on the frontlines in the Body of Christ. However, I believe *the local churches* are on the frontlines. The local church is the missionary's lifeline. Without the church's support, missionaries would have a tough time fulfilling what God has called them to do.

Strong local churches that preach Christ provide the foundation for reaching a community or town for the Kingdom of God. This is one reason why pastors need profitable people to serve with them in the ministry.

The truth is, in order for the pastor to fulfill the plans and purposes God has given to him, he *must* have people who are profitable to him for the ministry. The apostle Paul understood that fact. In Second Timothy 4:11, he wrote Timothy, *"Only Luke is with me. Take Mark, and bring him with thee: FOR HE IS PROFITABLE TO ME FOR THE MINISTRY."*

One of the meanings of the word "profitable" is *to be of service to*. Why is it so important to be of service to the man of God? Because God's desire is to have strong local churches that meet the needs of His people. However, if pastors don't receive the necessary help from their congregations, they will be limited in what they can do for the Kingdom of God.

What about you? Are you of service to *your* pastor? I pray that through this book, you will be inspired and motivated to become profitable to your pastor as God intended for you to be.

CHAPTER 1

The Ministry of Helps In the Local Church

Each one should use whatever gift he has received to serve others, faithfully administering God's grace in its various forms.

— 1 Peter 4:10 (*NIV*)

As I minister throughout the country, I often ask congregations, "Are you profitable to your pastor? Can your pastor say the same thing about you that Paul said about Mark in Second Timothy 4:11 — that you are *profitable* to him for the ministry?"

One of the meanings of the word "profitable" is *to be of service*. So I also ask people, "Are you of service to your pastor? Are you an asset or a liability to him? Are you a blessing or a curse? Are you a servant or someone who always shows up after the work is done?"

If you desire to be profitable to your pastor, you must be willing to faithfully serve people in your local church and community. That's what First Corinthians 15:58 is talking about when it says, *"Therefore, my beloved brethren, be ye stedfast, unmoveable, always abounding in the work of the Lord, forasmuch as ye know that your labour is not in vain in the Lord."*

Think about it: If Jesus needed disciples to help Him, it stands to reason that pastors today would need our help in serving in the local church. The truth is, pastors are always in need of good, quality help. They can all use a helping hand from time to time. Therefore, everything we do for our pastors should be done in excellence.

God Rewards Faithfulness

Here's another thing to consider: The twelve disciples trained with Jesus in His earthly ministry before they ever had their own ministries. Likewise, it's impossible for you to be successful in your own ministry without first having served in the ministry of helps because *God rewards faithfulness* (Matt. 25:21).

Remember, God is a God of order (1 Cor. 14:40). You may be called to pastor. However, you don't get saved one day and pastor a church the next day. Instead, God wants to see if you'll be faithful in small responsibilities, such as cleaning the church restrooms, working with children, singing in the choir, or setting up chairs.

Then once you pass that test, God will begin to add greater responsibilities to you. For instance, He may give you the opportunity to run the church bookstore or serve as an usher captain. As you continue to show yourself faithful with these greater responsibilities, the day will come when God lets you know you're ready to begin fulfilling your call to full-time ministry.

That's why serving in the helps ministry not only blesses your local church, but it benefits *you* as well. You see, as you serve the congregation alongside your pastor, you are planting seeds for your own ministry. When it's time for you to enter into full-time ministry yourself, God will reward your faithful service to your pastor by sending people to serve *you* faithfully.

That's why it's vitally important to take care of another man's vision and ministry as though they were your own. You see, the Bible says you will reap what you sow (Gal. 6:7). If you sow bad seeds of neglect or slothfulness into someone else's ministry, you will reap a bad harvest when it's time to launch out into your own ministry. But if you sow good seeds of diligence and faithfulness into someone else's ministry, you will reap a good harvest in your future ministry.

GALATIANS 6:9
9 And let us not be weary in well doing: for in due season we shall reap, if we faint not.

So if you sense a call to the full-time ministry, make it a priority to get involved in the ministry of helps right now. As you serve with your pastor, be creative in your area of responsibility. Believe God for new ideas. Never take any task, job, or responsibility lightly.

Make sure you give your all every time you do something to help in your church. If you are ushering, strive to have the best-looking section in the church. If you are a nursery worker, strive to be the biggest blessing to the kids. If you are a parking lot attendant, direct traffic with the joy of the Lord. If you are a sound engineer, have the best acoustics around. If you are a greeter, greet everyone with a smile. If you are a custodian, make your church the cleanest church in town.

Work as though you were serving the Lord Jesus
Himself. As Colossians 3:17 says, *"...whatsoever ye do
in word or deed, do all in the name of the Lord Jesus,
giving thanks to God and the Father by him."* When
your motive is to serve the Lord, you'll do everything to
the best of your ability, and God will reward your
effort.

The Vital Role
Of the Ministry of Helps

Let's look at a biblical example of the ministry of
helps in the local church.

ACTS 6:1-4
**1 And in those days, when the number of the
disciples was multiplied, there arose a mur-
muring of the Grecians against the Hebrews,
because their widows were neglected in the
daily ministration.**
**2 Then the twelve called the multitude of
the disciples unto them, and said, It is not reason that we should leave the word of God, and
serve tables.**
**3 Wherefore, brethren, look ye out among
you seven men of honest report, full of the Holy
Ghost and wisdom, whom we may appoint over
this business.**
**4 But we will give ourselves continually to
prayer, and to the ministry of the word.**

The twelve apostles were under direct orders to
take the Gospel to the world. They couldn't forsake the
mandate of the Great Commission to serve tables. To
solve this problem, they told the rest of the believers to
choose seven men of honest report who were filled with

the Holy Ghost and wisdom. These seven men would operate in the ministry of helps as they made sure everyone was fairly served at mealtimes.

Just as in the Early Church, today's pastor or minister shouldn't have to stop flowing in the supernatural in order to handle situations regarding the natural ministry of helps. Instead, faithful men and women who are of honest report and filled with the Holy Ghost and wisdom should rally around their pastor to take care of the practical matters of ministry. In this way, the pastor will be free to follow without hindrance the plans, purposes, and pursuits the Lord has given him.

Now let's see what resulted from the willingness of those seven men to operate in the helps ministry as the apostles ministered the Word.

ACTS 6:7
7 And the word of God increased; and the number of the disciples multiplied in Jerusalem greatly; and a great company of the priests were obedient to the faith.

Because faithful men did their job of waiting on tables, many more souls were added to the Kingdom of God. The apostles were able to continue fulfilling the mandate of the Great Commission given to them by the Head of the Church, the Lord Jesus Christ.

The same thing happens in the local church when those in the ministry of helps do their part and flow together as a team. They enable their pastor to give himself continually to the Word of God and prayer. This leads to more fruit for God's Kingdom as the lost are saved and the congregation's spiritual needs are met.

'Hold Up Your Pastor's Arms'

In Exodus 17:9-13, Aaron and Hur helped Israel win the battle against the Amalekites by operating in the ministry of helps. When Moses held his rod in the air, Israel prevailed. When his arms became tired and he stopped holding up the rod, the Amalekites began to prevail. So Aaron and Hur stepped in to help Moses. They stood by their leader's side and held up his arms for him until Israel had won the battle.

God is looking for more men and women today in the Body of Christ who will "hold up their pastors' arms," just as Aaron and Hur held up Moses' arms until the battle was won. In other words, God wants faithful people to surround and serve their pastor in the ministry of helps, thus making it easier for him to minister the Word to his congregation.

You see, when you usher, you're holding up the pastor's arms. When you work in the church bookstore, you're holding up your pastor's arms. When you work with the children, you're holding up your pastor's arms.

You should also continue to hold up your pastor's arms when you're not at church. For instance, when you're tempted to question your pastor's decisions, you should hold up his arms by determining *not* to talk against him in front of other brothers and sisters in the congregation.

Also, whether you're at home or at the workplace, you should continue to hold up his arms by praying for him and his family without ceasing. This is a very important aspect of being profitable to your pastor and an essential ingredient to the success of the church and his ministry.

Prayer is the backbone of any successful work for the Lord. It should be a way of life for us. In fact, First Timothy 2:1,2 reminds us that we have a responsibility to pray not only for our pastors, but for all those in authority over us.

Someone once asked a minister if he spent a large amount of time in prayer. He answered, "I don't often spend more than a half hour in prayer, but I never go more than a half hour *without* prayer."

That's the way it should be for each of us. We should live a life of prayer. Our pastor should be on our daily prayer list. And we should take advantage of each opportunity to be a part of our church's prayer group.

I've heard many preachers say that when they're physically tired, the anointing to minister to people is not as strong on them. This fact alone should be enough to motivate us to serve in the helps ministry. If one of our loved ones ever had a serious need, we'd certainly want our pastor to be able to minister to him or her as effectively as possible.

As the congregation serves alongside their pastor in the ministry of helps, the pastor can lead his flock the way the Lord intended instead of wearing himself out trying to fulfill both his and the congregation's responsibilities. He'll be able to minister to the people's needs without concerning himself with a lot of practical problems, such as finding enough nursery workers for the midweek service or enough parking lot attendants to direct traffic on Sunday morning.

A pastor shouldn't have to engage in the time-consuming, energy-draining chore of begging and pleading every week for help in the various areas of the helps ministry. He should spend his time doing what he's supposed to do — ministering to his congregation. But that's only possible as the people in the local church do their part, serving to the best of their ability in the ministry of helps.

CHAPTER 2

Honor Your Pastor

*And he gave some, apostles; and some,
prophets; and some, evangelists; and some, pastors and teachers;*
*For the perfecting of the saints, for the work
of the ministry, for the edifying of the body of
Christ.*

— Ephesians 4:11,12

God has blessed the Body of Christ with the fivefold ministry gifts. We should honor all the ministry gifts the Lord has placed in the Church — and that includes pastors. Pastors are gifts from the Lord to the local churches, charged with the responsibility of perfecting the saints for the work of the ministry.

The Lord has given this responsibility to the pastoral office, as well as to the other ministry gifts, so the Body of Christ can be edified. God's desire is to have strong local churches, but the local church is only as strong as the pastor. Therefore, it's essential that a congregation give their pastor honor, love, and respect.

15

Render Honor to Whom Honor Is Due

Writing to the church at Rome, Paul emphasized the importance of honoring those to whom honor is due:

> **ROMANS 13:6,7**
> **6 For this cause pay ye tribute also: for they are God's ministers, attending continually upon this very thing.**
> **7 Render therefore to all their dues: tribute to whom tribute is due; custom to whom custom; fear to whom fear; HONOUR TO WHOM HONOUR.**

Honoring men and women of God is an extremely important principle because honor is an attribute of love. Whomever we honor in life, we respect; whomever we respect, we value.

You receive much more from your pastor when you honor the office in which he stands. So never take your pastor for granted. Always treat him or her with respect.

You honor your pastor when you recognize and acknowledge that he is a gift from the Lord to you and to the Body of Christ. You honor your pastor when you don't talk against him or the decisions he has made for the local church. You honor him when you pray for him as one who is in authority over you (1 Timothy 2:1-3).

Another way to honor your pastor is to help serve those whom the Lord has entrusted to him, as recommended in Hebrews 6:10: *"For God is not unrighteous to forget your work and labour of love, which ye have shewed toward his name, in that ye have ministered to the saints, and do minister."*

It's a blessing to serve alongside your pastor in the ministry. Serving builds character in you as a believer. It's also important to develop a good relationship with your pastor. But you have to remember not to think of him as just "one of the guys."

It can actually be detrimental to become too familiar with your pastor. Too much familiarity can cause you to respect him less than you did when you first met him. So remember, when it's time to enjoy fun and fellowship with your pastor, then have fun and fellowship. But when it's time for business, it's time for business!

Submission vs. Agreement

Keep in mind that the Lord has given your pastor the authority to stand in his ministry office. Always remember who is in charge. Realize that your pastor has to make decisions and operate the church the way he believes the Lord is leading him. As Hebrews 13:17 says, *"Obey them that have the rule over you, and submit yourselves: for they watch for your souls, as they that must give account, that they may do it with joy, and not with grief: for that is unprofitable for you."*

People usually don't have any problem with their pastor as long as they're in agreement with his decisions. But the first time the pastor makes a decision they don't like, they often decide they do have a problem with him.

But there's a difference between submission and agreement. When you're in agreement with something, you don't have to bring yourself into submission. It's only when you *don't* agree with something that you have to consciously make a decision to submit to the person in authority over you.

1 TIMOTHY 5:17
17 Let the elders that rule well be counted worthy of double honour, especially they who labour in the word and doctrine.

You must continue to honor your pastor, whether you're in submission or in agreement with him. Your pastor is working on your behalf. He's on your side. The Lord has equipped him for that office. He has a responsibility both to you and to the Lord, and you help him fulfill that responsibility when you honor the office in which he stands.

The Cost of a Lack of Honor

There's a price to pay for not honoring the men and women God has placed in the ministry offices. People who lack honor may go through life without having their needs met.

You see, you limit God's power from working on your behalf when you don't honor your pastor or the other ministry gifts God has placed in your life. We can see this principle in action in Mark's account of the time Jesus visited His hometown Nazareth.

MARK 6:1-6
1 And he went out from thence, and came into his own country; and his disciples follow him.

2 And when the sabbath day was come, he began to teach in the synagogue: and many hearing him were astonished, saying, From whence hath this man these things? and what wisdom is this which is given unto him, that even such mighty works are wrought by his hands?

3 Is not this the carpenter, the son of Mary, the brother of James, and Joses, and of Juda, and Simon? and are not his sisters here with us? And they were offended at him.

4 But Jesus said unto them, A prophet is not without honour, but in his own country, and among his own kin, and in his own house.

5 And he could there do no mighty work, save that he laid his hands upon a few sick folk, and healed them.

6 And he marvelled because of their unbelief. And he went round about the villages, teaching.

Because the people in Jesus' own hometown didn't honor him, no mighty works were in manifestation. The people asked, "Isn't this the carpenter, the son of Mary?" They didn't see the office Jesus was standing in, nor did they acknowledge the anointing of the Holy Spirit upon Him. They focused in on His humanity rather than on the office of the prophet of God.

Verse 6 says Jesus marveled because of the people's unbelief. Unbelief came into manifestation because there was no honor for the prophet of God.

The Pharisees and scribes also didn't honor and recognize Jesus as the Messiah. As a result, they couldn't receive from Him either. They stopped the power of

God from flowing to them because their lack of honor manifested unbelief in their lives.

Similarly, when we don't honor our pastors, unbelief takes the place of honor, and mighty works cease to manifest in our churches. Where there's no honor for the men and women of God, there can be no mighty works. *No honor — no mighty works.* This is an important phrase to remember.

You limit the power of God from flowing personally to you when you don't honor your pastor. If you choose to only see the human imperfections of the person instead of the dignity of the pastoral office in which he stands, you hinder yourself from receiving the Word of God from him. You also hinder the power of God from working on your behalf.

Today many people refuse to receive the Word of God from other ministers in the Body of Christ because of the ministers' race or gender. But believers should always esteem the office and the gift God has given each individual rather than judge the person by his or her appearance. This truth is confirmed by what Paul said in the book of Galatians:

GALATIANS 3:28
28 There is neither Jew nor Greek, there is neither bond nor free, there is neither male nor female: for ye are all one in Christ Jesus.

Honor God by Honoring People

The Holy Ghost manifests Himself where He is honored. You also receive more illumination and guidance from the Word of God when you honor and reverence

the Holy Spirit. Therefore, if you grieve the Holy Spirit
instead of honoring and reverencing Him, you keep
Him from manifesting Himself to you in your life and
ministry. That's why Ephesians 4:30 warns, *"And
grieve not the holy Spirit of God, whereby ye are sealed
unto the day of redemption."*

How do you honor the Holy Spirit? One way you
honor God is by honoring people. First Peter 2:17 says,
*"Honour all men. Love the brotherhood. Fear God.
Honour the king."*

People can tell how you feel about God by the way
you treat other people. So if you want to touch the
heart of God, serve and honor people. And remember,
no honor — no mighty works!

CHAPTER 3

Bring Your Tithes
And Offerings
Into the Storehouse

Will a man rob God? Yet ye have robbed me. But ye say, Wherein have we robbed thee? In tithes and offerings.

Ye are cursed with a curse: for ye have robbed me, even this whole nation.

Bring ye all the tithes into the storehouse, that there may be meat in mine house, and prove me now herewith, saith the Lord of hosts, if I will not open you the windows of heaven, and pour you out a blessing, that there shall not be room enough to receive it.

— Malachi 3:8-10

W hen I started tithing in my local church, I thought I was doing great. But a few months down the line, the Lord began to show me that giving offerings was just as important as paying my tithes. (Offerings are what you give over and above your tithes.) I was tithing faithfully, but I wasn't giving offerings faithfully.

'That There May Be Meat
In Mine House'

We often put more emphasis on paying our tithes than on giving offerings. But in Malachi 3:8, the Lord said He was being robbed, not only in tithes but in offerings as well. God wants to have meat (finances) in His house because He wants each pastor and congregation to fulfill the plans and purposes He has established for that local church.

When there's a lack of finances, a church is limited in what they can do for the Kingdom of God. But when there is meat in God's house, effective youth and children programs can be established. When there is meat in the house, the church can support missionaries. When there is meat in the house, they can feed the poor in their community. When there is meat in the house of God, one church can impact the world.

Besides the cost of its various outreach programs, the local church itself has many expenses, such as light, water, gas, sound equipment, repairs, etc. All these needs of the local church are met through church members' tithes and offerings.

A church that's struggling every month to keep the doors open won't impact the community the way it should. A local church can only have the life-changing impact God desires it to have when there is meat (finances) in His house. Therefore, it's essential that every member of every local church gives tithes and offerings to promote the Gospel of the Lord Jesus Christ. This is an essential part of being profitable to one's pastor.

Bringing Our Time and Talents
Into the Storehouse

We should not only be willing to bring our tithes and offerings into the local church, but we should be willing to give of our time and talents as well. In Acts 9:36, we read about a sister in Joppa who was full of good works and busy serving the people of the city.

ACTS 9:36
36 Now there was at Joppa a certain disciple named Tabitha, which by interpretation is call Dorcas: this woman was full of good works and almsdeeds which she did.

Dorcas used her talents and gifts to bless many of the people in Joppa. Her talent was in the area of sewing. The Bible says she made coats and garments for the people of Joppa.

ACTS 9:39
39 Then Peter arose and went with them. When he was come, they brought him into the upper chamber: and all the widows stood by him weeping, and shewing the coats and garments which Dorcas made, while she was with them.

You can follow Dorcas' example. Whatever the Lord has anointed and blessed *you* to do, do it with joy. Love can be expressed in so many different ways, such as cutting grass, cooking, cleaning, praying or giving someone a ride to work. Discover your talent, and be a blessing where you are.

A great place to start is right in your home. Sometimes it is difficult to serve the people you live with because they often take you for granted. But if you endeavor to be a blessing to them, God will bless you.

In Luke chapter 10, Jesus mentioned one of the greatest acts of serving found in the Word of God. It is usually referred to as the story of the Good Samaritan. We can learn valuable lessons from this story.

LUKE 10:29-37
29 But he [a certain lawyer], willing to justify himself, said unto Jesus, And who is my neighbour?

30 And Jesus answering said, A certain man went down from Jerusalem to Jericho, and fell among thieves, which stripped him of his raiment, and wounded him, and departed, leaving him half dead.

31 And by chance there came down a certain priest that way: and when he saw him, he passed by on the other side.

32 And likewise a Levite, when he was at the place, came and looked on him, and passed by on the other side.

33 But a certain Samaritan, as he journeyed, came where he was: and when he saw him, he had compassion on him,

34 And went to him, and bound up his wounds, pouring in oil and wine, and set him on his own beast, and brought him to an inn, and took care of him.

35 And on the morrow when he departed, he took out two pence, and gave them to the host, and said unto him, Take care of him; and whatsoever thou spendest more, when I come again, I will repay thee.

36 Which now of these three, thinkest thou, was neighbour unto him that fell among the thieves?

37 And he said, He that shewed mercy on him. Then said Jesus unto him, Go, and do thou likewise.

Because the Good Samaritan had mercy and compassion on the injured man, he went out of his way to help him. We could say he went the "extra mile" and beyond! When the man Jesus was talking to commented on the Good Samaritan's act of kindness, Jesus told him to "Go and do likewise" (v. 37). We should be "doing likewise" today as well.

For many people, it is easier to give some of their money than it is to give of their time. The Good Samaritan gave of his money *and* his time to help the injured man. He bandaged the man up and gave him a ride to a nearby hotel. He checked him into the hotel and took care of him through the night. In the morning, he paid for the man's hotel expenses and told the host of the hotel to take further care of the man. He also told the host that he would reimburse him if any expenses exceeded the amount of the money he had given him at the start.

As Christians, we should go on a manhunt, so to speak, looking for opportunities to help hurting people just as that Good Samaritan did. I once heard a preacher say, "I would rather *see* a sermon than *hear* a sermon." We are to be living epistles to the world (2 Cor. 3:3), so we cannot afford to let opportunities to serve people pass us by.

The Good Samaritan in Luke 10 walked in the love of God and didn't miss the chance to do a good deed for someone in need. That made him a candidate for God's promise in Psalm 41:1:

1 Blessed is he that considereth the poor: the Lord will deliver him in time of trouble.

Do you want to be a candidate for that divine promise too? Would you like God to deliver *you* in times of trouble? Then become a *giver*. Give of your time, your talents, your energy, and your finances to your local church. As you do, you'll not only become profitable to your pastor, you'll be abundantly blessed yourself!

CHAPTER 4

Know How To Flow
With the Spirit of God

*"For what man knoweth the things of a man,
save the spirit of man which is in him? even so the
things of God knoweth no man, but the Spirit of
God."*

— 1 Corinthians 2:11

A person who knows how to flow in the supernatural things of God is a person who is profitable to his pastor.

In these last days, I believe God is calling the Church to a higher level. It's time to lay aside the weights that have beset us so we can climb higher and go deeper in the same realms of the Spirit that the Early Church tapped into. God wants spiritual men and women — people who know how to flow with His Spirit.

Spiritually Mature or Carnal?

Therefore, it's important that we keep our minds renewed by the Word of God so we can *remain* spiritual men and women of God. We must endeavor not to let envy, strife, and divisions keep us apart — the very works of the flesh that hindered the Corinthian church from experiencing the supernatural things of God.

> **1 CORINTHIANS 3:1-3**
> **1 And I, brethren, could not speak unto you as unto spiritual, but as unto carnal, even as unto babes in Christ.**
> **2 I have fed you with milk, and not with meat: for hitherto ye were not able to bear it, neither yet now are ye able.**
> **3 For ye are yet carnal: for whereas there is among you envying, and strife, and divisions, are ye not carnal, and walk as men?**

Today we have the same manifestations of spiritual gifts in the Body of Christ as the Corinthian church did. We also still have envying, strife, and divisions. For instance, some believers still refuse to worship with other believers because of their skin color.

But if we're going to flow in the deeper things of God, we can't remain in the same spiritual condition that hindered the Corinthian church. We have to lay aside divisions and move on to the "spiritual meat" of what God has for us.

The apostle Paul could not speak to the Corinthian church as spiritual men and woman because of their carnality. They weren't ready to receive the meat of the Word.

Likewise, we cannot walk as mere men and women of the natural realm if we want to be profitable to our pastors. We must walk as spiritual men and woman in order to be profitable in these last days.

God Would Not Have Us Ignorant

God doesn't just want *ministers* to know how to flow with the Spirit of God; He also wants those who serve in the ministry of helps to flow in the supernatural. A layperson should be able to flow in the Spirit just as his pastor does.

Many people think that because they work a secular job or because they're not called to the fivefold ministry, they can't walk in the deep things of God. But a layperson can also minister God's power to others and flow in the gifts of the Spirit. Just look at the biblical example of Stephen.

ACTS 6:3-5
3 **Wherefore, brethren, look ye out among you seven men of honest report, full of the Holy Ghost and wisdom, whom we may appoint over this business.**
4 **But we will give ourselves continually to prayer, and to the ministry of the word.**
5 **And the saying pleased the whole multitude: and they chose Stephen, a man full of faith and of the Holy Ghost, and Philip, and Prochorus, and Nicanor, and Timon, and Parmenas, and Nicolas a proselyte of Antioch.**

Stephen was one of the men chosen to serve tables in the Early Church. He served in the helps ministry, but he still flowed in the supernatural power of God. The gifts of the Spirit were in manifestation in his life.

Verse 8 says, *"And Stephen, full of faith and power, did great wonders and miracles among the people."* Stephen preached the Word and operated in the gifts of the Spirit. He was powerfully used by God Almighty, even though he was appointed as one of the overseers in charge of the practical business of the Early Church. Stephen had other responsibilities besides ministering the Gospel, but God still used him to flow in the Holy Ghost.

You also can be profitable to your pastor in this capacity. You can serve in a supportive role or work a secular job and still flow in the power of the Holy Spirit. For example, even though you may not be called to the fivefold ministry, you could visit nursing homes, jails, or hospitals to minister the Word of God and flow in the gifts of the Spirit.

God doesn't want any of us to be ignorant concerning spiritual things. In First Corinthians 12:1, the Holy Ghost said through Paul, *"Now concerning spiritual gifts, brethren, I would not have you ignorant."* God expects us to become spiritually mature so we can carry out His plans and purpose here on the earth.

It takes a spiritual individual to flow in the things of the Spirit because they are *spiritually* discerned. It takes a person who is filled with the Spirit of God to discern the things of God.

Learning To Flow
With the Holy Spirit

Every local church should be pastored in the supernatural. God wants His people to be sensitive to the diversities of the gifts of the Spirit (1 Cor. 12:4); the differences of administrations of the Spirit (1 Cor. 12:5); and the diversities of operations of the Spirit (1 Cor. 12:6).

The Holy Spirit should always have free course in the local church. He is always willing to manifest Himself to meet the needs of people. He *wants* to manifest Himself to the Body of Christ.

Some of His responsibilities are to lead us, guide us, comfort us, speak to us, and show us things to come. And the more we learn how to discern His voice, the easier it becomes to flow with Him.

I personally learned how to flow with the Holy Spirit when I began to minister to other people through street witnessing and visiting hospitals, nursing homes, and jails. While ministering to people, I began to become acquainted with the voice of the Holy Spirit.

You will also get to know the Holy Spirit personally as you minister to hurting people. But if you're not doing anything to help people, He has little reason to manifest Himself through you.

God wants to use you. But if you don't make yourself available to Him, He won't push Himself on you. You can learn so much about flowing with the Holy Ghost by making yourself available to minister to people. When you desire spiritual gifts because you love people, the gifts of the Spirit will begin to manifest for the people's sake.

This is also a good way to learn how to be led by the Spirit. In the end, you will become a great asset to your pastor. The Holy Spirit will keep you busy. But remember, He is a Gentlemen. He won't force you to do anything you don't want to do.

The Holy Spirit continually manifested Himself through the earthly ministry of Jesus and the disciples because they were busy ministering to people. So if *you* want to learn how to flow with the Holy Ghost, start ministering to hurting people. As you do, flowing in the Spirit will become second nature to you.

Each church service is a learning experience for me. I endeavor to stay sensitive to the Holy Spirit to see how He's going to manifest Himself in the service. For instance, if there's an anointing to heal in the service, it's usually discernible.

You, too, have the responsibility in a church service to stay hooked up with the Holy Spirit and with your pastor until the people's needs are met. For example, suppose the pastor invites people to the front for prayer. If the singers are singing, you should be singing along with them. If the pastor asks the congregation to pray for the people who came forward, you should be agreeing in prayer that the people's needs would be met. (When I'm ministering to people in a prayer line, I ask the congregation to stretch out their hands while they pray as a point of contact.)

You should *not* be holding a conversation with another person about something else during this time in the service. It should be a quiet and reverent time because someone is experiencing a special time of personal ministry.

You will grieve the Holy Ghost if you don't honor His Presence. Therefore, you should develop your spiritual sensitivity so you can know when He wants to move in a special way in a service. Train your spirit to know the manifestations and moves of the Spirit of God.

Come to Church Expecting

A minister can do no more than what the congregation allows him to do. Therefore, it's very important to come to church *expecting* God to move. You create an atmosphere of faith when you come expecting.

Just like a hungry man who comes home after a hard day's work expecting to receive a good meal, you should come to church expecting to receive from the Word of God after dealing with the affairs of life all week. You actually draw on the gift within your pastor when you come to church expecting. An atmosphere of expectation causes the pastor to stir up the gifts God has placed within him.

So come expecting to have your needs met. Come expecting your circumstances to change. Come expecting to receive illumination from the Word of God.

Paul instructed the Corinthians church to both follow after love and to *desire* spiritual gifts (1 Cor 14:1).

When you desire something, you want it so much, you expect something to happen that would cause that desire to come to pass. For instance, when I walk in a room and turn on a light switch, I *expect* the lights to come on. In the same way, when you come to church, your "expectors" should be turned on, causing you to earnestly and confidently *expect* to receive from the Lord.

My college economics instructor used to tell us, "When there is a demand for a product in the economy, more of that product has to be produced to accommodate the needs and desires of the consumers. For example, if the demand for Coca-Cola increases, more Coke has to be produced to meet that demand."

Likewise, when you come to church expecting, you place a demand on God's power to meet your need, which causes more of that supernatural power to be produced. When you come to church expecting, you put yourself in a position to be blessed.

So if you're sick before coming to church, come expecting to be healed. If you're depressed before coming to church, come expecting to be refreshed. If you're bound before coming to church, come expecting to be set free!

A Final Word

I pray this book has been a blessing to you. My prayer is that it will inspire and motivate you to become a more profitable person to your pastor, to your local church, and to the Head of the Church at large, Jesus Christ.

If your desire is to attain God's highest for your life, you can't have a more worthy goal than to strive to become more and more profitable to God's Kingdom. Just keep in mind this one central truth: If you want to be *great in the Kingdom of God*, you must *serve the people of God*.

About the Author

Rev. Byron August was born in 1964 in Donaldsonville, Louisiana, and at the age of eight, accepted Jesus Christ as his Savior. Inspired by his grandmother, Byron began a life of serving and has been very active in the helps ministry ever since.

When Byron was eighteen years old, he began attending a Full Gospel church. Eager to embrace every opportunity to serve people, Byron performed janitorial duties, worked in the church bookstore, and visited nursing homes and jails. After proving himself faithful to serve, he was appointed to oversee various areas of the church's helps ministry and outreach programs. In addition to these duties, Byron also taught a Sunday school class and served as a deacon in the church.

In 1984, Byron graduated from Nicholls State University in Thibodaux, Louisiana, with an Associate of Science degree in general business. Later, he prepared for ministry at Rhema Bible Training Center in Tulsa, Oklahoma, graduating in 1990.

Then in 1992, Rev. August took a sixteen-month sabbatical to serve as a missionary to Lima, Peru, in South America. While on the mission field, he ministered in various churches throughout the country, taught in a local Bible school, and worked in a local missions station. He also met and married his wife, Dr. Sylvia August, who now serves alongside him in the ministry.

Rev. August is a licensed itinerant minister who conducts services throughout the United States and Latin America. He and his wife Sylvia reside in Broken Arrow, Oklahoma, with their children: Daniel, age 5, and Victoria, age 1.

For Further Information

For additional copies of this book
or for further information regarding
Rev. August's ministry schedule,
please write:

Rev. Byron August

P. O. Box 2833

Broken Arrow, OK 74013